I0489028

©DENNIS MBUGUA

Reviewer:

Peterson Njagi, PhD

Contents

CHAPTER ONE

NUGGETS OF GROWING YOUR BUSINESS

There are lot of myths and misconceptions out there that are being spread out by the media regarding entrepreneurship that I would like to dispel. The most common one is relating entrepreneurship to financing. The reality is that entrepreneurship does not equal financing. In other words, you don't need financing to start of your entrepreneurial journey. All you need to know and do is to identify a problem in the market place that people will be willing to pay you to solve for them. This now validates entrepreneurship to having customers, revenues and profits; it's all you need for you to start off which also defines entrepreneurial success. The process of building a business without any external funding, that is, being strategic and efficient with your money so your business is self-funded is called bootstrapping. Bootstrapping is always a good technique anyway.

There are a few major pillars on bootstrapping that include:

a) ***Customer acquisition*** which is primarily about generating revenue, making profits and influencing the positive side of the equation. A common mistake done by most startups is waiting to be fully ready by having everything in place for them to approach or get in contact with their first potential client. This is usually a wrong move by business owners as it tends to postpone the period in which they would sign their first contract, and line up more prospects in their pipeline for them to start generating revenue. The reality of entrepreneurship is that you should start thinking of your first customer before your product is even ready. The fact in business is that most sales are made on a promise rather than a demonstration. You

   may have to show your potential clients some or all of your marketing material but when signing, you don't have to be ready to operate on a full scale. When you make your first sale, act fast, get your product ready and deliver it as soon as you can.

You cannot afford to bootstrap while waiting for everything to be ready before you start prospecting, booking appointments with potential customers and making sales. You need to make yourself as visible as possible in the market place and start positioning your value as soon as possible. This way, you will start gaining feedback from your customers which you need for product improvements. This is vital as they pay you for your product(s) and/or service(s) you offer therefore giving you an opportunity to start generating revenue to grow your business.

For instance, if your business does development of huge and complex product(s) for other businesses, it's advisable that you get to work hand in hand with an interested company that would want to be an early adopter for the potential of seeing their problems solved. Develop for them a tailor-made product that would exactly fit their needs at a low price. This is a bonus for you as you would have a customer on board who would give you feedback and improvement points as you generate some revenue for your business instead of working on assumptions. As a collateral benefit, you'll see how good it feels to make that first sale and moving from concept to business. It's a great way to start off than working in a bubble until the product is ready; there is no logic in working blindly. Not all companies, though, are interested in this model as they may have pressure and perhaps, they would want a product that is already working right away.

b) *Managing spending* which is more on influencing the negative side of your financial equation, that is, the expense (money going out). Find out all the significant costs your business incurs and keep them under control. The most common types of expenditures include office rent, your salary and that of your employees, services from professionals like accountants, and lawyers etc. and of course getting a top-notch website and business cards for your business which makes you a lot credible and competitive. Before spending money, you should ask yourself if it will be generating business and paying for itself in a direct way. For example, you need to determine why you need an office before you want it. If you are a start-up and your business needs demand that you must have an office, you could share an office space with a group, use business accelerators (free spaces for people in the same industry) or share space with other companies. It's very uncommon that clients would come to your office as most of them would want you to visit their work places to present your goods and/or services to them; always be willing to save them the travel time. If you can work from home, which is by far the cheapest option without interfering with anyone or without mixing your work and personal life, is much better. Stories of many successful companies today started off in the kitchen, or in the living room. All in all, get all the necessary tools and equipment you need to run your business. Do not save on the important stuff.

Again, most companies tend to pay their suppliers a month after delivery of services, which is not a bad thing if it works for both of you. You just don't want to pay the supplier immediately after delivery when your client pays you after a long time of sending an invoice. Always manage the time at which everyone is paid. Asking customers to pay on the invoice date without offering them an extended payment period is a nice way to get your customers to pay earlier. On the other hand, negotiating for a longer payment plan with each of your supplier is an ideal strategy so you don't have to advance the money from the production stage to the final payment by the client. Negotiating for favorable terms is important for both your customers and suppliers.

While bootstrapping your business, you should be interested by the total amount of money you spend today. Pay for what you need now.

c) ***Having the right competency acquisition*** is absolutely important for every startup. In this case, competency could mean people or money. Some services could be outsourced while others could be kept in-house. In the early life of a company, it a challenge to pay for all the services you need and therefore the cheapest way to handle this is through battering with others. For example, your business is in the professional photography and you need accounting services. You could as well exchange your services with an accountant where you do some services for the accountant and you get their services in return. This is an effective strategy for your business and plus you are able to build a good relationship with the other parties.

Another classic way that is affordable for companies to get professional services they need is through giving equity to its employees. This is basically giving some company shares to employees such that even if the company succeeds in the future, they have an opportunity to make up for it as the company shares increases tremendously. The advantage of this is that an employee can get a share of the profit of the company and shares of a company. It's important to note that shares of a company have value and during the first years of the company, a few shares may increase exponentially to huge sums of money. Success stories of the same can be witnessed when Google and other large companies were just starting off and employees received shares when they were still small, years later, the employees became millionaires. If employees believe in your project and your mission, it's a great thing for them and your business venture in the long run.

If you are looking for a cost-effective way to get critical competencies for your project to take off, it's a great idea to partner with someone who is in the same situation just like you. They could be a co-founder in your venture and usually they have no salary at all but in exchange of shares. Even down along the road as you will start sharing profits, you will still need to see the value of the partnership. This is a much better way to get started than never to start because you cannot afford to pay a salary.

If you are not after enticing competencies with shares as a tool, you can use paid employees in the short term while considering variable payments as an option. Variable pay usually ties compensation to performance. The benefit of this is that compensation will be tied to the success of your company; when times are good, it goes up while when times are bad, it goes down. This works out best when you set a fraction of their compensation as fixed salary that you would at least be able to pay them at the end of every month and have the variable part to their compensation which ultimately depends on their achievement and a certain level of performance which could be based on an individual level or a group level. It's a moral code for your business to ensure that people who are on your variable pay have an objective that they can directly influence so they stay motivated and have to freedom to decide on what they are able to make.

On the other hand, variable pay is a great way to limit the salaries of your employees while starting your business and slowly getting their pay to increase as the company continues succeeding. This is best achieved when it's defined at the start since most employees will be okay to work with low salaries as they slowly reap the benefits with the success of the company. In every situation, I find variable pay as ideal for everyone in your company as it will motivate them to produce more since they can work harder and earn more. This may also nurture the entrepreneurial spirit in them.

d) *Customer retention.* Sometimes it's not always easy to retain an existing client due to external factors that you may not be in a position to control them. Often times, there is always something that can be done to retain a customer when you realize the much-needed effort to gain new customers. It's a lot harder with only a twenty percent chance of gaining a new customer today. Always try to understand why your customer may be willing to take the time and effort to look for a new vendor by spending a significant time into making phone calls, exchanging mails, one on one meetings or even better, making a point of meeting with the vendor before they select one. It's usually a painful move when a customer changes habits and its best practice to always try and see if you can do something about it to help change the situation whenever possible. This may be a very good feedback which could be extremely helpful for other customers as well.

Building customer loyalty is a vital means of getting new customers and retaining them. When you are able to retain existing customers, they will bring you referrals, buy more from you and write you quality reviews that will help your business scale. It's usually the best way and it requires the least amount of investment. Focus more on customer loyalty through complimenting them, taking time to knowing them and be willing to do an investment that will make them happy, like gifting them and constantly making improvements in ways you do your day today business.

e) *Managing your business* involves having the mechanisms needed to stay on the right track. Mostly, spending too much time making decisions or potentially going to the wrong direction, which results to the massive waste of money, is the number one killer of start-ups. Every entrepreneur makes, and will make, mistakes; they are a part of doing something and the least you can do is to learn from them. If you are going to make a mistake, you better do it early so you can learn from them and adjust accordingly.

For instance, when developing a product at first, most things are usually assumptions based on your experience and that of others and it's by no means a guarantee that those assumptions are right or will work out. The best and real way to confirm your assumptions is to create a minimum viable product that is effective with key features then getting in contact with a customer for feedback. Refined feedback for your product is called version 2.0 because it's the one that has been tested by your customers who paid for it and they expect an outcome. Version 2.0 will always have a big chance of success than the previous one. With that being said, avoid thinking too much about the future and focus on having your product to the market as soon as possible. Now that you have a chance to know this as you are reading this book, neither should you hesitate to contact your customer nor procrastinate like many entrepreneurs do. Meet with customers early on in the life of the project and get viable feedback. While developing your product and/or service, it's important to keep in mind that not all people will like what you offer, others will like it but will prefer certain changes or adjustments made on your product and/or service while others will be totally in love with what you offer.

The hidden cost of bootstrapping is time as a factor of production. When you take care of the minutes, the hours will take care of themselves. Always set and work with deadlines for your projects and once you achieve try to analyze and evaluate the outcome and where you compare to your plan. This help you keep track of what you are doing and gives you a chance to reflect more on the next steps. Learn to set a clear and measurable objective and always choose the best use of your time.

Also working in short cycles will make you adapt and be strongly connected to your feedback as competition will start proposing new things and your customer's expectation and feedback will start to evolve. It will also give you a chance to test the assumptions of your business plan which may be as a result of historical performance, industry statistics or even guess work. Many entrepreneurs tend to think that their ideas are the best and that they have no competition, or it's the most innovative (which can be), therefore, they end up doing guess work on their business plans. They fail to understand that their product can be related to an already existing product, it could be an evolution of another product or it's a replacement of another product. It's way better to use the statistic of that product in your business plan than doing complete guess work. In case your product assumptions end up more positive or more negative, it's important to take a step forward to investigate and understand why this would be happening as it may mean either that you need to potentially adapt your plan and make things work out as fast as possible or slow down and reorganize things.

As an entrepreneur, you should also avoid the significant work process that generates significant extra costs for your business. This work process is the fact that business owners tend to wait too long which means spending more money on the operations of the business. For instance, paying salaries, rent and more of everything before even realizing if they are headed for the right or wrong direction. However, if they are in the right direction, fine, no money has been wasted.

There are two things that may weigh your business down besides the initial start cost. The first one is salaries and the second one is the challenge in knowing the time it will take to sign your first customer and get paid.

f) **Having a good work-life balance** since most of the time you will be working a lot. It's important to draw the boundary so that your vision is not blurred at best and that you are able to make the difference in your venture. Creating time for your loved ones and tagging them along in your projects is important for you. You need to build a business and have a life, I mean, your business should give you more enjoyment, and more life.

With bootstrapping, it's possible to build a large company (unicorns) and have a wonderful life. It's a common myth today that you need external financing to build a unicorn. Do not buy into that, it's false. Classic examples of unicorns are Zoho and Right Technologies. They were built as a result of bootstrapping. Today, we are in the unicorn and the economic bubble. The sweetest thing about bubbles is for you to come out before they pop. If you can do this, your company can be ultra-successful.

Bootstrapping using services is much better as opposed to products because products are scalable. The best scenario for this is when your service contract and your project are of synergistic instances. That being said, it's easier to offer a service contract where for instance, you identify a problem for a customer and you decide to build a product solution for them, and then you include a requirement in the contract where a client will pay, say monthly as opposed to waiting for a couple of months. This is a strategy to build cash flow as you will get paid along the way as the customer funds the project.

The most powerful way of bootstrapping today is when you are doing another job (having a day job paycheck). Companies that use this methodology tend to break even a lot earlier especially when their business is generating revenue and it's covering costs. Now, the major and a big concern with this is that you are basically doing two jobs. These are tradeoffs that business owners need to rethink especially when you have a family that needs your nights and weekends. If you don't have much obligations and family commitments on this, then you can take the tradeoff. Do not quit your day job yet until your business cash flow supersedes your salary and that your business now needs a lot of your time and attention. It's important to understand that it takes some time, probably a few months to raise capital for your business, so, you'd better think twice before quitting your job.

On the other hand, if your employer is okay with you doing a side business, then good for you. Some companies do support their employees to think outside the box and grow. Some employers even go to an extend of raising seed capital for their employees with visions. Not all employers really do support this.

The ultimate challenge is when you are starting or doing a business in the space that your employer is venturing thereby becoming a competition. Most employers wouldn't tolerate this kind of behavior within their company. All in all, it's always important to check your employment agreement and see if it prohibits entrepreneurship.

Can A Small Business Compete with A Big Business?

This is definitely one of the most frequently asked questions and the answer turns out to be a yes. A small business usually has a lot of fear when they hear about a big business but the reality is that a small business can actually beat a big business because they have very specific competitive advantages that a big business cannot touch.

The first one is that, as a small business owner, you can quickly change the product experience for a customer and personalize the experience to an individual customer. From experience, this makes a customer happy and you are able to serve them faster. This is usually not the case with big businesses because they will take a lot of time as there are usually a lot of politics which may hinder performance.

Secondly, when it comes to social media marketing, a small business is able to get personal with customers even when they write a review. To a customer, it feels like a real human being as opposed to big companies which may not be able to give a personalized experience because they are kind of wooden in how they do it. Small businesses can have relatively lower budgets for social media ads as they will tend to focus more on targeting valuable customers. Big businesses, on the other hand, will spend huge budgets on ads.

Finally, it's because a big business has big needs. Sometimes small business owners think, *"Awe if we only had this much in sales. If only we increased the size of our company, we wouldn't have problems anymore."* The reality is that, that's just not true. Money is always an issue in business. It's just that, with big businesses, it's bigger, and they have more paperwork, it is usually very time consuming for them.

Common Mistakes Made in Entrepreneurship

One of the most common mistakes made by new entrepreneurs is giving free-away. In the real world, you don't get real feedback from your customers with free products and/or services because there is low expectation as many of us have with free things. Say for example, you build an application, a website or anything and give it away free for a period of time then turn it to premium. It's worth noting that it's very difficult to convert free to paid. Another crucial factor is that financing it for the set period of time will be a lot more difficult because there are high chances that there will be no revenue and most likely there will be no any external funding. This idea will only work best if you are super rich and you can afford to give things away for free. If you are not yet, stop dreaming and start building traction to the market place!

Most businesses start with an exit strategy which usually ends up as a lie. When starting or running an existing business, do not anticipate to be bought out by a big company. It's important that you build and execute your idea(s) first because for you to even be bought by a large company, you must be at a level of having a huge market opportunity and having characteristics of fast growth. In reality, very few big companies buy out other companies in a year. Do not play the low probability game, focus on what matters most.

Again, your business needs profits to sustain it, therefore you need to find a way to create cash flow. An error that most businesses make is to build a company that frequently requires cash injections for it to survive. In reality, a business should be designed to be profitable, and self-sustaining, meaning, it should thrive on its own. This is incredibly important for your business survival as it will keep you and your business going.

A frequent common mistake seen by most entrepreneurs is they see raising capital as an end rather than as a means. If you manage to raise capital from investors, it does not mean that you are successful or it's an end of the road. It simply signifies the beginning of a new journey. You will most likely have pressure to perform your action plan and frequently report to investors with progress and deliver results.

Another error that most entrepreneurs make when they receive funding is that they start allocating big salaries for themselves right away. Remember, investors will always want a return on investment for their money and by you receiving a small salary is a means for you to contribute to the company's success as the rest of the money goes to other activities. Always hold the shares in your company dearly as you are sitting on a virtual pile of money and when you ever sell it someday it will turn out to be real pile of money.

What You Need to Know
It's incredibly important to have a business model (how your business will make money) because this is what will sustain your business just like every other

business. When creating a business while bootstrapping, often times, you may need a business model a lot more than a business plan (a formal statement of business goal and plans for reaching them). This is so because it's a mistake that most entrepreneurs make to have a wishful thinking in their business plans and they end up getting numbers and forecasts out of the air. Informed investors do know this fact and that's why they stress more on having a sustainable business model. This is a great way to perfect your pitch as it's important to analyze and validate your business by identifying the customer's pain points, how much they are willing to pay, and the model that will work best; whether it's lamp-sum fee, subscriptions, or transactional fee. Profitability is a requirement for your business's health and its success.

When to Consider Getting an Investor

The best time for most businesses is when you have everything set in place. It's always better and fulfilling when investors start reaching out to you with an interest to invest in your company. This happens only when you have a real and a functional business model that actually generates you profits to sustain your business. This may take a bit of time as you will need to understand your industry and market, the many terminologies that you will encounter along the way, product market fit and much more. This is why bootstrapping is so important.

The olden days when you could present concepts to investors and they would be willing to fund it are gone. Today, investors fund real businesses, not concepts. My advice for entrepreneurs is not to create a business plan when starting off their businesses (unless you can't do without it). Instead, focus on creating a prototype (minimum viable product), get all the important stuff done and focus on the core elements that will trigger attention. This is where the rubber meets the road and all the facts stand out on whether your project works or not; all the hallucinations and fictions in your business plan go away at this stage. It's a huge plus in getting your prototype in the market place where real people actually get to test it and give real feedback. See, when you do this, whenever you will go to investors, you don't have to convince them to trust you, but instead, you will tell them that it's tested and proven in the market place. You need to build a business before seeking any funds.

For your plans to happen as expected, your assumptions have to materialize in the real world.

However, not all companies are financeable and this is not to say that they don't succeed. The reason for this is because venture capital model is usually designed for very specialized class of companies which will portray some special characteristics like growing at an exponential pace and addressing large market opportunities. Very few companies show these characteristics.

Pitching

Pitching is a universal skill. A time will come when you need to pitch yourself, idea, or project. You need a quick and effective process to nail the pitch. When pitching, always know that most of people usually don't have the time to listen in long and probably boring conversations so try to make your presentation short and sweet. Always know that the chances of you closing a deal or landing a huge business opportunity are slim to none, so always have an open mind and make them engaged and intrigued by turning from monologue to dialogue so that you can get yourself to the second round of conversation; that's the goal. Every conversation should always be leading to a destination. Talking about the relevant experiences and/or transferable skills like being a quick learner, agile or ability to work under pressure show that you are bringing something on the table. The reason why most people don't get venture capital funding, or don't get hired is not because they are unqualified or unskilled, it's because they are not convincing and therefore, they do not get the benefit of doubt. It takes practice and a bit of work to perfect your pitch.

Dealing with Investors

There are many ways out there of doing valuation of your company and many times it's more of an art than a science but as you may already know, that when negotiating with an investor, it's at the best interest of an entrepreneur to have a high valuation of the company and the best interest of the investor to value it low. It's always important to discuss this matter because at the end of the day it should be a win-win case scenario. Knowing what stake you are giving away is crucial because for example you agree that your company is worth $1,000,000, then if you divide it by 100, then you know that one percent of your company is worth $10,000. In the same vein, if you could be raising $1,000,000 for 35% of your shares, this would mean that after you've successfully raised $1,000,000 you will be owning 100 percent minus 35% of the company, or in other words, will be left with 65% of your company, and your investor will own 35% of the company. Investors will often times prefer to invest money in your business step by step (in milestones) which is a good choice by far for both of you. By this I mean, the higher the price of share, the more money you will get. Let's say for example that you are trying to raise money through selling equity in your company. Instead of raising $1,000,000 with 40% of your shares, you could raise $500,000 with 20% and later on, another $500,000 with only 10%. Or maybe even 5%. So, in the end, getting the same $1,000,000 for 25% of your shares instead of 40%.

Secondly, milestones open doors for you in case you may undergo a phase of development that may not generate revenue for a period of time and this will focus on putting your product and/or service in the market place.

Finally, some investors do seed investment which focuses on start-ups that have barely started while some on the development of start-ups that have shown and proven to be a profitable and a sustainable business model. With this in mind, milestones are mutually workable.

When pitching to a potential investor for your business venture, always remember that they should always bring something in return to your business more than just money whenever possible. For instance, it could be training your staff, help increasing customer base by referring your business to their network or help in the marketing of the product and/or service, handling the management of the business or even bringing their own skills that would take your business to the next level. For every move you make in terms of giving equity away to an investor, there should be a concession in return. Not all money is good money.

While business plans are not always required in every business case scenario, you may find the need of having one for your business and therefore it's important to note that it's just like a map which helps you to stick to the right direction and stay focused so you can achieve whatever you set in your mind at the beginning. *Here are some elements of a good business plan which include:*

1) Having specified targets like two or three that you would like to achieve within a specified period of time, say on quarterly basis.

2) Measuring and tracking the key performance indicator which include cash in hand (how much do you have in the bank), your net profit in the last quarter and finally how much do you pay yourself as a business owner every quarter. That is where you get to know and understand how healthy your business is becoming.

3) Analysis of your most valuable employee for the business by looking at their profiles.

4) Defining clearly the most valuable product(s) and/or or service(s) line(s) in your business out of the ones that you offer. Knowing what percentage of sales fits that profile helps in staying more focused.

5) Identifying the most valuable customer for your business by defining the profile of the best possible person to do business with your business. What are their demographics, what are their psychographics, what do they look like and act like, and then what percent of sales, roughly, fit into that category?

6) The most valuable message which is a summary, in just a few words, of the reason why people do business with you. And that's why it becomes the basis of your marketing message. Also measure what percent of your overall marketing shares this message. Is it focused in your marketing, or a little bit scattered?

7) A harvest strategy which relates to you in terms of what you get daily, weekly, monthly, and yearly out of your business. It also defines what the ultimate harvest is. The idea is that you continually move forward in your business, and you're always getting some reward for the hard work and effort that you're putting into it.

Why Raise Capital?

The reason why a business venture may need to raise capital before starting off is because of the development process of the product, the launch of the product in the market place, to overcome barriers to entry in the market, or just the need to grow the company at a fast pace to gain strategic benefits from being a market leader by building a stronghold. All this should always require a significant amount of funding. Just know how much you need; this means that you need a very good understanding of your business. You should be able to answer questions like how your business is going to make money, how long will it take to acquire a new customer, what are the daily expenses for your business, whether you are going to invest in something along the way, and how long will you take before you realize your first dollar. Once you are able to answer questions like these, you will be good to go. There is no specific strategy for raising capital for your venture as each one of them is unique to your business, your personality, and the stage of development your business is currently in. Therefore, there are plenty of paths you can take and you should always choose the best fit depending on your business as there is no right or wrong answer. Some strategies involve giving a limited amount of information to the outside world at the beginning for fear of ideas being stolen. It's always important and fair enough to discuss your vision and why you think your business is going to succeed, and most importantly, the workability of your business model. If you are completely uncomfortable giving away any information and that it's a big no-no for you, then you should come up with strategies using sources of capital that do not require you to disclose any information. In real life, Online and consulting business will often require little capital as compared to the traditional brick and mortar.

There are four main way of raising capital for your business, which include:

1. **Selling equity.** This is where you sell some percentage of your company shares to an investor. It's a common way adapted by most businesses and the benefit of this is that you don't have to do the monthly repayments. The major drawback of this is that they will participate in key decision making of your business and that down the road, you will share profits and you may not be quite sure how much you will pay back for the investor money. A central element in this is a business plan.

   A great thing with equity is that you can do a lot of things with it and define exactly what the investor is entitled to. This is for example, important when selling shares to someone close to you such as friend or family. Those are people who might not necessarily bring the advice and mentor-ship, network and/or customers that you would expect from regular investors along with the money they give you. You can therefore sell them shares that give no voting rights, which means, that they can claim a portion of the profits of the company as every other investor but will have no way to make decisions for the company or participate in its strategy other than trying to convince you to do something.

2. **Debts.** This is yet another way to get your business to start-off. With debts, you know how much it will cost you, and you might as well start to pay off as early as possible maybe on a monthly basis, which may at times weigh down your finances heavily. If you are relying on debt, you better be generating enough revenue in a fast pace to service your debt. Most people do not like debts but it's a great way to keep investors away if you can afford it and if debt is what you want. Once the loan is paid back, you and the lender can each go your own way and never meet again. No strings attached unlike equity.

You should always be able to manage personal loans incase things don't go as planned otherwise I advise you against it. If you have personally taken the loan, then the institution from which you got it can go after you relentlessly until they have gotten from you the last penny for that loan. Since your company is a different legal person, it can get loans from all types of institutions, and would therefore be the one that the banks or other institutions would go after to get back their money. If that company is a limited liability company, then the most that can happen is to lose the capital you originally invested. That's a safe way to take on debt to fund your company.

Note the difference between straight debt and convertible debt. Straight debt is the basic loan that you and I are used to getting for our personal needs.

The money you borrow is to be repaid over a certain period of time. Or at the end of the period with a certain level of interest rate. That's a great way to get capital easily.

On the other hand, convertible debt is different from straight debt only in the fact that there is an added element in the contract that states that the lender can either receive his money back with interest or the equivalent amount in shares of your company at a certain point in time.

3. **Personal finances.** At least you must put something of your own before getting people to believe that they can put their own in your business. It's the first and foremost, plain and simple. Raising your own capital is a sign that you are convinced before you convince others and it's also the most logical way to raise capital. You could get capital from your own means or from family. Putting some money of your own in your venture gives you credibility in the eyes of investors.

In any case, you should like that option, because it will first be a great way for you to get a much better return on investment than any other investment out there. It's a great way to start your company without sharing any of the control and ownership of the company just yet.

4. **Revenue from your business.** This is by far the best and the cheapest means. When you have paying clients for your business already, you do not necessary need all the mentioned above. This way, the business will be funding itself as it grows. It's bootstrapping!

Should You Share Your Idea?

Honestly speaking, when it comes to sharing of your business ideas, it's advisable that you share out with the world. Many tend to overrate the true risk of sharing and have the reflex to keep the idea to themselves. This behavior tends to happen because you want to be the first one to hit the market. There is a huge disadvantage for this because you may get a few sales here and there at the beginning and competitors will very quickly join you in offering the same product and/or service and before you realize, you have no benefit from having to be the first.

Also, spending too much money early on is not wise enough because the idea has not been tested and you have not seen how the market responds to it. Being the second or the third to enter the market could be a good move as you will see first-hand how the market responds and what to adjust.

Secondly, there is a very slim chance that your idea will be stolen for logical reasons and you should not keep it so much to yourself that you hinder your own development efforts. However, this does not mean that you go telling your idea to everyone or walk around with a sign explaining your idea or business model on your back. The truth of the matter is only few people would be concerned to stealing your idea because the mass majority won't bother. Maybe only one percent will take some time to think about it. Out of the one percent, the other one percent will do something about it or even execute it. That means that only one person out of ten thousand that you are going to tell your idea will steal; the probability is almost zero. So, don't panic. When your business thrives, you will likely start attracting the eyes of a lot of individuals, and companies that want a slice of your market. A lot of competitors will come popping around you and only the fittest ones will survive.

On the other hand, while you may be shying away from sharing your idea with investors, as much as they have the means to steal it, they are actually interested in investing in businesses that demonstrate ability to return back their money big time. All in all, I don't think that you should refrain from sharing your idea with investors, friends and family.

QUESTIONS:

i. What is bootstrapping?

ii. Entrepreneurship does not equal _____

iii. What are some pillars of bootstrapping?

iv. Explain how small businesses compete with big businesses

v. Why should you share your idea?

vi. Why do investors prefer milestone investment?

vii. What are some ways of raising capital for your business?

viii. What are some common mistakes entrepreneurs make?

ix. What is the difference between a business plan, a business model and a minimal viable product?

CHAPTER TWO

THE DO'S AND HAVES FOR EVERY BUSINESS

Vision and Values

A company's vision is primarily like a destination of where your business will be in the future. It motivates you to make decisions every day to move you closer and closer to that destination. It also motivates your employees, because they feel like they're a part of something. When coming up with a company's vision, you need to ask yourself questions and answer them with your first impression. Some of these questions include what are we doing in terms of sales? How big is our business? How many locations does your business have? How many employees do you have? Where do you see your company five years in the future? Where are your business locations, if you have multiple locations? What is your geographic reach? What kind of customers are you serving? What kind of products and services do you offer? What do your facilities look like? Do you have a certain kind of uniform or personal branding for your employees? What kind of technology does your business have? How do you attract new customers? How do your employees act like? What is the day-to-day culture of this future business? How does your operations give you a competitive advantage? What other thoughts do you have about your future business? These are just but examples. You can use your own wordings, questions or format. The bottom line of asking and answering questions is trying to describe the future as much as possible such that someone else can see it in their minds. A company's vision can always be changed or updated as long as it remains powerful and motivational that it can be used to create or represent culture in your business.

Vision and values go together as the foundational document of creating culture in your business. The vision describes the destination of where your business is headed. The values, on the other hand, describe how we're going to get there, what is it that we believe in, what are we going to use as our operating method in getting there. Systems are important to have in a business because they tell people what they should do and how to do it. The problem is, we don't want people to act like robots. We want them to be able to make their own decisions, and values fill in the gaps that give people guiding principles to make their own choices when things aren't clearly described in systems. Be clear by defining the words in your values as they may be very subjective because one word may mean something different for me and you. A company's vision is more like fingerprints; they are all unique. Once you have the values, they now become the basis of hiring, motivating and training employees.

Money alone isn't the only consideration for your business. Does selling that product and/or service, help you with living those values? Does it support those values? And how much do you enjoy offering that product and/or service on a scale of zero to ten? zero being it's absolutely miserable and ten being it's the most enjoyable thing you can possibly think of. This seems like a strange question, perhaps, but it's not. It's very common, for business owners to drift a little bit into selling a product and/or service, that doesn't really support what they value, simply because they were chasing money in the moment.

Always ensure that your vision develops a culture that emphasizes collaboration, transparency, and accountability.

The Most Valuable Line

Identifying your most valuable line of products and/or services as a business owner is key to understanding your business better. It's absolutely important especially if you are offering a variety of products and/or services. It requires for you to analyze your business keenly. This is called the entrepreneur math which means it's just subjective. It helps you in getting clearer what you should be focusing on. The idea is to focus all of your efforts, all of your sales, all of your marketing into selling that one thing that is the most valuable line, because not only will that bring the most profit to your business, but that will bring you the most enjoyment, as a business owner. It's not a matter of giving up something you love so much as giving up something you love for something you love more, and putting more time, attention, love and care into something that really gets you going. Hesitation for most business owners is fear, fear of loss of money since every dollar counts especially for small businesses. It's not so much what you may think that losing up lines that are less valuable will have you less money. You may lose a little money initially but you will far make up for it. You'll be happier. You'll be able to market to them better, because you're not weighed down selling a product or service that really isn't bringing much value to your business. This is all about focus and the more that you can focus on your most valuable line, the more profitable your business will be and the more you'll enjoy the day today reality of being a small business owner. By the new customers that you get, who are buying you most valuable line, you'll be able to devote more attention to them. However, if you are only offering one thing, you don't need to analyze because it's that one.

Employee(s)

As a business owner, it's important for you to understand that you are an employee of your own business venture and that you are the most valuable and the most productive person in your business. You shouldn't therefore treat yourself the opposite of what you would treat that employee who is simply amazing as they devote to the success of the business by working long hours, bend backwards to make customers happy and do whatever it takes daily to make that business succeed. You should reward yourself too. Many business owners tend to develop the philosophy of paying themselves last of what remains within the business. This is not a healthy choice for the long-term success of your business. Of course, you want to leave some profit in the business to help it grow. But you also need to have long term stability in the business by rewarding yourself, as the business owner. You also want to see that reward, that salary, progress and increase over time.

There are ways to determine how to pay yourself a salary which include:

i. Talking with an accountant as they are the right people because they are aware of the laws in your country with regards to compensation. They will even help you figure out the appropriate ratio between dividends versus salary.

ii. Start with paying yourself something even if the amount is very low. That becomes the baseline of your salary and your dividends can grow. It's easier to start with something small then increase over time. This will allow you to realize progress.

iii. Ensuring that all your basic needs are taken care of, and so are your personal inventories. That should form the basis of you monthly salary as your business continues to evolve.

iv. Consider what it would cost to replace you with that superstar employee who does what you do. You are that kind of superstar employee putting in that kind of effort. What it would take for them to be attracted to come work for your business and that's what ultimately you should be paid as a business owner. This happens for most mature companies that have been further down the road and make more profits.

Deploying Employee Loyalty

In a small business set up for example, the biggest expense is usually labor; the costs involved in hiring. A lot of business owners make a big mistake of hiring fast which is an expensive mistake in the long run. Essentially, this should be a slow process so that you are able to get the best fit for a particular position. Today, it's important to build employee loyalty; people who love working for you as this will help in realizing increased lower turnover. It will also save you from all the expensive processes of advertising for the position and the time of taking them through the hiring process just to get the right fit and also the training process for them to be familiar with some of their duties. Therefore, it's way cheaper and much better to be with employees you already have and not considering to replace them. Considering that you may alter customer loyalty because people just don't like change and would like to be seeing the people they are used to. It's a painful experience when you lose customer loyalty by failing to build employee loyalty. On the other hand, the expertise of your employees always grows in their positions and this will facilitate for passing on of the skills to others. This way, leadership is also nurtured as good employers will always want to see employees rise through the ranks so it becomes easier for them to exit the business in the future. That said, employee loyalty is a big factor that when you pay more attention to it, it will have more dividends for your business in the long run.

When discussing about employee loyalty, this is a two way round effect because for them to be loyal to you, you have to be loyal to them as well. With that I mean, you look to taking care of their families and genuinely care about them because they can always feel it. This does not mean that you overlook mistakes because as a leader, you should always correct mistakes and expect great performance. Also, providing them with some benefits like medical insurance and retirement plans is a good thing and it will make your employees stick around. It's worth noting and understanding that employee loyalty is always just not about money as increasing pay has just a little effect on the whole concept of loyalty and this is where most business owners go wrong. This does not therefore mean that you oppress them by paying lower rates. Their pay should ideally be in the same range as the market rates of people doing the same kind of job they are doing. Employees are motivated by money up to a point where their basic needs are taken care of. Having random rewards for them as opposed to predicable rewards can also have a great impact for your business because they will be more motivated. Random rewards could be gifts, perks, vacations or other things that come unexpected. For instance you could tell people *"If you get 100 of these sales, then you get a vacation,"* that's actually not very motivational, but if you say, *"For every sale you make, you get a raffle ticket, and we're going to have a drawing at the end with a variety of prizes."* that keeps everyone engaged, even the people who perform in the average, because they feel like they still have a chance. Employees like to see progress in themselves and in your business, therefore, you should create an ample environment for them to have professional and emotional growth. Everyone likes being part of the winning team. You can now see that it's the little things that build employee loyalty.

Sharing your business profits with employees is not a good idea because it has a low or no motivation at all except if they are sales people. If you decide to do profit sharing, you will realize that during low times in your business, you pull it back. If you have to do it, just do it gradually over time rather than retracing your steps.

When you think about sharing equity with employees, you have to be very strategic and careful with that move because it's not going to increase employees' motivation in any way and again it's something that you cannot take it back easily. Ideally as a small business, you should focus more in growing your company as shares will gradually grow. Equity sharing best happens with big companies that do not feel a pinch since they have millions of shares so it's no big deal to give away a share to one or two employees.

Working with Remote Employees

Pros

Depending with the nature of your business, working with remote employees (someone who does not work physically in your office and may be in a different country or part of the world) may have some huge advantages for your business especially if you are tech savvy because you probably won't need an office so there will be no overhead costs of operations. Secondly, you will also have a pool of talents to choose from beyond your country of residence. This may be less costly on the rate of paying them since some may have the flexibility of working from home or as a result of the difference in the economy. Finally, development of talents may be the outcome when you give people the flexibility of working from their own homes since most employees really enjoy this. This will make them want to stay with you more.

Cons

Remote employees may not have the value of interacting with each other and this affects the business culture of your company. Now that you have the opportunity to hire employees from different parts of the world, you may experience severe challenges especially when it comes to accent. Different people have different accents and this may be detrimental especially when the role involves dealing with a client who is from a different part of the world and may not be familiar with the accent. Secondly, when hiring from a different part of the world, you may have challenges of time zones and again let's say you have hired from a developing country, you may experience electricity challenges of power black-outs from time to time. Finally, building employee loyalty is almost impossible in this type of set up because there is no physical interaction.

Firing Employees

This is always a tough thing to do but it's an essential part of running a business. Employees who perform poorly may perform well in another company and this is usually an opportunity for them to grow their careers. Also, underperforming employees should be removed as this will help other employees perform better. However, you should consult a legal advisor with regards to laws on terminating employees for the region you are operating your business from. *On that note, I will give you four steps that will make termination of an employee less painful. It's called the four-strike system.*

1) The first step when they do a mistake is to ignore and let it go because when people often do a mistake, they feel bad about it and would like to correct it so let the growing process occur.
2) The second step is to point out the error by telling them that you have noticed something unusual therefore making it a pattern rather than an occurrence. In addition, with the verbal correction, you could ask the

employee, *"What steps could I take to help you do better with this?"* That puts you in a position where you're a helpful resource, rather than a taskmaster. Try to engage them in a dialogue to explore how to improve their actions. Then, follow up with them and hold them accountable for making the change.

3) If they don't show any improvements, give them a written warning and issue it to them personally and also discuss with them about it. Use a standardized system and file the written record as it will cover you legally when it comes to dealing with employees. Again, you can ask them, *"What can I do to help make sure this does not happen again?"* Build an action plan together, and do what you can to help them follow it.

4) The forth step is to let them go because of the consistent type of behavior they are not correcting. You owe it to them, you owe it to yourself and you owe it to all the other employees in your business to let them go. Do not look for excuses to keep them any longer as there is never a convenient time to dismiss someone. At this stage, they should surrender any materials that may be security liable to the company including laptops, phones bought by the company and so on. And if the person had access to keys or passwords, change all of them.

Skills Necessary for Business Growth

There are three important skills that every entrepreneur should have for their business to grow. These include:

A. **Sales** which is an act of persuading people to do what is best for them. This is usually an achy word for many but the reality is that no business on the planet today can survive without making sales because nothing moves without a sale, from everything you have to the products and/or services your business is offering. If you are not selling or you hate sales, you better change your mind set for you to go to the next level. Today, it's better for a company to have a sales team rather than a management team. Sales team do generate revenue for the survival of the company. Don't get it twisted, selling isn't pushing or pressuring people, it's about sharing great and valuable information with people and most importantly, nudging them.

Sales is the always profession of all times and when you can master the art of selling, you probably won't need a job especially if you are creating your own product and/or service. A salesperson is an independent business unit that has the potential to control his/her financial destiny therefore making it the highest paying profession. Unfortunately, how to sell is not taught in schools and even sadder, very few companies train their sales team on core things like blocking customer objections, prospecting, following up, building trust, qualifying clients among others. The good news is that you as a salesperson or a business owner can always take time and learn it on your own and grow your income over time. Do not be afraid to learn and practice selling, remember it takes courage to make money and when selling, your level of conversation will determine your level of income. You therefore must learn to take conversations your way.

A key to selling is making your customers happy by giving them what they want and at times doing more than they expected. People buy from people they like and more so, people they trust. This is what will keep your business going especially if you are starting off. However, it's important to know that not all customers were created equal. By this I mean it's important to identify your most valuable customers. Whether you have some customers already or not yet, just take time to think on who is or who you would like to do business with. Identify their commonalities in terms of demographics, that is, what is their general age range? Which gender do they lean towards, male or female? What is their general income? Where do they live in terms of geography, and what other features demographics wise do they share in common? Now keep in mind that when you're hiring people, you don't want to discriminate based on age or gender. In a marketing context though or when identifying your customers, not only is it appropriate, it's absolutely necessary because we want to focus all of your marketing, all of your sales on a particular type of person. Take a keen look at their psychographics. Psychographics simply represent what's going on in their head. What's their psychology? What are the activities that they share in common? What is their interest? What kind of hobbies are they involved in? What opinions do they have or do they lean towards a particular political party or another? What are their attitudes about life in general, and what values do they share in common? By clearly identifying your most valuable customer, you'll make it easier to sell to them, to cater for everything about customer experience to their unique needs. Identifying your most valuable customer is the foundation for running a successful business.

There are a lot of places that you could position yourself to go for the most valuable customers and quality leads when prospecting. Some are Off-line like identifying where they gather for different events. This will help you out in knowing your marketing and advertising budget. An Online way is by finding out which social media platforms they use as this will give you an idea of where you should spend your time on. Remember that, money and power always follow attention so you need to make the most of it in getting yourself out there.

Secondly, it's building everything in your business around what they want. Figure out what every single touch that they have with your business and act accordingly by putting much of that into the business and you will eventually start attracting those kinds of people naturally.

The third way is to partner with businesses that are already doing a great job in attracting your most valuable clients. Know that they are a complimentary to your business and not a competition. For instance, some financial planners partner up with accounting firms who are serving the same kinds of customers. What you can do is cross-promote each other's businesses. Refer clients to each other.

The fourth way is to always qualify clients by asking the right questions which will lead you to knowing things like if indeed there is need and urgency, whether they have the budget and the time needed, and most importantly if they trust you.

B. **Marketing** is getting your message out there to your target audience. There are so many ways to get your message to a mass audience including using billboards, media advertisements, use of the Internet via social media, blogs and forums among others. Marketing is more of a science than an art and therefore it's important to test and identify which one works best for you depending on the nature of your business and you will get a good idea on which ones you should capitalize on and which ones to just leave them alone. There are also important elements of your marketing which include:

　　i. *The place/location of your business.* This is an important factor when it comes to choosing your business preference. Sometimes a change in place can lead to a rapid increase in sales. You can choose to sell your product in many different places. Some companies use direct selling, sending their salespeople out to personally meet and talk with the prospect. Some sell by telemarketing. Some sell through catalogs or mail order. Some sell at trade shows or in retail establishments. Some sell in joint ventures with other similar products and/or services. Some companies use manufacturers' representatives or distributors. Many companies use a combination of one or more of these methods. In each case, just make sure you pick the right location that works best for you.

ii. ***The product that your business is selling.*** Having a great product for a business is a huge plus because customers want a return on investment and most importantly, value for money. It's therefore important that you develop the habit of continually examining and re-examining the prices of the products and services you sell to make sure they're still appropriate to the realities of the current market. Sometimes you need to lower your prices. At other times, it may be appropriate to raise your prices. Many companies have found that the profitability of certain products or services doesn't justify the amount of effort and resources that go into producing them. By raising their prices, they may lose a percentage of their customers, but the remaining percentage generates a profit on every sale.

iii. ***Price*** is a major factor when it comes to selling your products to clients especially for small businesses or when introducing a new product and/or service. There are four ways in which you can come up with the price of your product. The first method is called *price penetration* which is where you look at what the market is charging for similar products and/or services you are offering then you come up with a lower price. This will result in having many clients but with lower profit margins.

Secondly, it's the *market pricing method* where you look at what the market is charging then you charge around the same price range.

Thirdly is the *cost-plus method* where you calculate the cost of production then you include for example a 30, 40, or even 50 percent markup depending with whichever percentage you want to use of what was the cost of production.

The fourth way is the *Gabor Granger Pricing* Technique which is based upon asking people the likelihood of them purchasing a product or service at different prices. For example, you perform an experiment and let's say you invite ten people in a room. Then you ask them that how many people would buy if the price was X, let's say seven people say that they would buy. Then you increase the price to say X+1 then you find out that say, five people would buy. By using this formula, you will end up with a price that best works for you.

In the pricing methods discussed above, choose the one that fits best for your business depending on the product and/or service you are offering, your skills and/or talents, and also the market you are in.

Knowing when to raise or to reduce price is a very important factor in your business. You may have heard of stories where someone raised their prices by 100% and they increased sales by 500%, or maybe they lowered their prices and that resulted in an increase in sales. Raising or lowering prices for your products and/or services depends on five major determinants which include:

- *Inflation.* For you to stay on top of inflation rates, you have to know the rate of inflation of the country you are living or operating your business in and this usually changes from year to year. Different countries have different rates so it's a reality in life and in business and so you must be aware of what is happening when it comes to inflation in your market.

- *Costs of material or labor* involved which may either increase or decrease. Always keep a close eye on that because you want to make or continue making profits. For instance, if costs increase and you keep your price the same, your profits will decrease.

- *What your competitors are doing in terms of pricing* matters a lot. As much as you want to stay competitive, your competition may want to undercut you by charging less prices. My advice for you is not to involve yourself in price competition especially if your business is small. It's the called the death spiral in pricing because when you set a certain lower price, your competitor sets a much lower price and the competition continues downwards. Of course, you do not want to compete on basis of prices alone. It's crucial that you provide and position more value rather than lowering prices.

- *The demand of your products and/or services in the market.* Over time as you will be in business, demand for what you offer will grow in the market place and your waiting list will start being longer. Sometimes you may realize that you will even run out of inventory. Whenever there is a waiting list, raise your prices!

- **_Experimenting._** Usually, you don't know for sure whether raising or lowering prices is going to lead to an increase in sales. So, the two most important words in marketing are _test it_. Give it a try. Offer the same product to two different groups at two different price points. And then measure which of the two were more successful. This is referred to as A/B testing.

_iv)_   **_Promotion._** This is an important role in business because regardless of the field you are in, you should always promote, promote, and promote all the time. You are always in the marketing business first because even if you have the best products and/or services in the world and no one knows about it, you won't sell. The most powerful means of promoting businesses today is over the Internet via the use of various social media platforms which may vary a lot in terms of popularity, email marketing, search engine ranking and so on. There are a lot of other means which are Offline like the use of newspapers, articles, magazines, billboards, fliers, and the use of network marketing among others. Promotion includes all the ways you tell your customers about your products and/or services and then how you sell to them. Small changes in the way you present, promote and sell your products can lead to dramatic changes in your results. Even small changes in your advertising can lead immediately to higher sales. Large and small companies in every industry continually experiment with different ways of advertising, promoting, and selling their products and/or services to their consumers. And here is the rule: ***Whatever method of marketing and sales you're using today will, soon or later stop working. Sometimes it will stop working for reasons you know, and sometimes it will be for reasons you don't know. In either case, your methods of marketing and sales will eventually stop working, and you'll have to develop new sales, marketing and advertising approaches, offerings, and strategies.***

C. **Branding** is how you present your message to the target audience. The core behind branding is story telling which help a lot in building brands and often times it pulls the attention of listeners and captures imagination. It also helps a lot in creating advertisements as you can use your story anywhere you are interacting with customers. Story telling also plays a major role in recruitment as employees would always want to be associated with a company that has a story behind it. A company's culture is also built on stories it is part of the identity of a business and it's also a very powerful training tool. When creating your company's story, make sure it's short so that it is easy to remember.

Secondly, make sure it's emotional so that people can connect with it and lastly, try to use vivid images as much as possible so it's easy to pop in people's minds. When writing a company's story, here are some questions

that can help you with that process. Where were you when you started the business? What was
going on in your life? What happened that caused you to say, *"Now's the time for me to be a business owner?"* What problems did you see needed solving, and that your business could solve for others? What challenges did you face along the way of being an entrepreneur? Do you have a customer story, an experience where a customer was so thrilled with their experience that they had to tell you about it? How about an employee story, something where they did something excellent for your customers? Or, perhaps you have an experience where you gave customer service above and beyond what was expected.

Another great way to building your brand is by becoming a great thought leader. When becoming a thought leader, you have to start from somewhere and climb the ladder. There are several ways to start off some of which are creating a blog or a podcast where you share great knowledge of your product and/or service with the world. You can also offer a free white paper, e-book, or a report, just something of value to your most valuable customers that they can download when they come to your website. Creating an Online following and consistently sending newsletters on a regular basis with tips and tricks that your customers will find valuable is a great way too. This will create a good relationship with your audience and potential prospects. You can even host or sponsor targeted community event whether Online or in your locality. Using videos as a way to build brands by sharing valuable content Online is a powerful means. The idea is to know where you and your business are at the moment and create a perception on being a thought leader. Find out the one that works best for you and build more and more on it for your company and brand. Always keeps in mind that you should build a brand that you yourself would buy. Ask yourself, "can you buy you?"

QUESTIONS:

i.   What is the importance of a company's vision?

ii. How will you determine how to pay yourself a salary?

iii. Explain how to deploy employee loyalty

iv. What are the advantages of working with a remote employee?

v.   Explain the four-strike system

vi. State and explain the three important skills for building a business.

CHAPTER THREE

EMBRACING THE DIGITAL LANDSCAPE

Unlike the olden days when Information Technology (IT) in an organization was to support business functions, today they do a lot more than just that as the digital landscape in various industries continue to evolve. The IT professionals are now for everything in an organization from hardware and networking to social media and data analytics. Every organization needs to take proactive steps in catching up with these trends failure to which they will be left behind in terms of productivity. The use of IT as a tool in your organization should be the heart of how your business interacts with its customers, sell to customers, enhance customer experience and deliver products and services. Historically, information technology leaders have been a lot more comfortable with tactic than they have been with strategy. This is because back in the day, IT was more of a support team/organization as they took orders from the rest of the organization rather than driving any significant part of the strategic priorities of an enterprise. The best run IT companies were those that could take orders quickly, fulfill them efficiently, and then move on to the next order. The key metrics for these IT organizations were ensuring that systems were up and running all the time, and on-budget delivery of projects. Today, IT is more core to business units and functionaries across the enterprise. The problem is, many large enterprises do not translate enterprise level strategy to business unit strategy as well as they should. For example, the enterprise may have a strategic imperative to grow revenue by 20% in the next fiscal year. Many organizations will not translate that into marketing role to grow that revenue versus sales role, versus the product and services areas roles, versus the merger and acquisitions department's roles. Or, if they do go about that, this is often not communicated to those outside of the small leadership teams in each business unit or functional area. Let's think of an example from your marketing department and your human resources department. The marketing department should develop a strategy that is externally focused. That is to say, the focus will be on your company's existence and potential customers. The HR department should develop a strategy that is internally focused. Meaning, it should focus on your company's employees. Information Technology, in contrast, needs to breathe life into those two plans and all plans in between.

You should have objectives for your organization that are overarching pursuit for the next three to five years. This include:

i. Goals, which are the quantifiable metrics that determine the degree to which an objective is being successfully reached.

ii. Tactics, which are the various actions available to a company that will help the company reach its goal.

iii. Measures, which are the quantifiable metric that determines the degree to which a tactic is being successfully pursued.

By doing these in your organization, in all divisions and/or business units, you as a business leader can see before anyone else where there are common needs articulated across the different parts of the company. Information Technology can again be the center of the conversation about how best to address those needs. It might seem presumptuous to push one's colleagues to formulate better plans and it may seem like a risk in some ways. When you do this successfully, you and your organization will be among the rare class of strategic change leaders who make things happen.

Call to Action

Developing change management plan, engaging a vendor if appropriate, implementing the plan, migrating old data from the old systems to the new systems, and finally shutting off old systems can seem so daunting that you might elect to kick the can down the road. Doing that means that competitors will go about the dirty work sooner than you and will be set up for great advantages that you will not be able to reap, and ultimately, you will fall behind. It's important to note that this undertaking is difficult in the modern day. The mantra of today's business leader needs to be simplicity. What does that mean for you in practical terms? I'd say, set standards for the biggest systems and hardware that you use, like email, PCs, tablets, phones, ERP, procurement solutions, business intelligence, and the likes. This may be a challenge if your company has multiple operating companies or business units associated with it, each with a bias towards using and doing their own thing. The key here is to present the benefits to simplicity in the form of cost savings and simplifying the integration of data. You should also consider reducing the number of vendors you engage in and choosing the best fit for every service they offer as this will reduce costs through economies of scale and also reduce the governance burden on your team. It's important to always monitor and validate the performance of each vendor.

Using cloud-based systems such as software-a-service solutions for your organization can be of great benefits including developing more rapidly scaling solutions, turning capital expenses into operating expense, and increasing the Information Technology team's financial flexibility in the process therefore, making it easier to access data. Isolate critical assets into separate enclaves are the words of Dr. Ron Ross of the National Institute of Standards and Technology. This idea has been used by many private sectors as well because it ensures data breach by one part of the technology does not lead to a broader breach. As you can already see, there are many long-term advantages for your organization as simplifying your technology portfolio can be a primary way to secure the enterprise. These are not easy steps to undertake, and it requires marshaling the right resources inside and outside of IT while creatively engaging the best vendor partners.

In the past, marketing departments would hire people with MBAs and marketing concentrations and maybe those who had marketing experience in other firms. This traditional way of doing things needs a major update because marketing department not only needs to hire personnel with a depth of knowledge in that discipline, but they also need to have technology experience as more marketing campaigns have a heavy emphasis on digital channels. Also hiring technologists with strong business acumen is a plus, as this will become increasingly important to ensure that there is a faster path to developing great ideas.

Today, every department in your company needs to be customer centric and be more cognizant of customer experience whether they have maximum or minimum direct contact with customers in your organization and Information Technology is at the heart of this change. Your organization needs to realize the vision of digitization by being flexible, quick to action, quick to cancel initiatives that are not working, iterative in approach and more collaborative. For example, sales teams need to have better digital details of the customers they are selling to. Likewise, your product and/or service divisions need to think about digital channels through which those very products and/or services will be sold. For your organization to realize its vision, your IT infrastructure should be clear and its strategy should be clearly defined.

Businesses today are competing in a supersonic speed, trying to out-do each other with the same interest of standing out and getting huge traffic flows of customers. However, as this happens, many businesses continue to lose more and more business opportunities to their competition simply because of a lack of knowledge or ignorance of today's modern digital economies and trends. Making your business visible by leveraging the tools for yesterday as well as today will set you apart from your competition and help you achieve your goals. You need a good operational strategy expertise with you to get you going. That said, here are a few tips on the modern-day digital trends that would take your business to the next level.

1) **Having A Simple, Well Thought Out and A Highly Functional Website for Your Business.**

Now, your website is the most valuable piece of digital marketing you will have. It will enable you to get access to millions of people. An effective website that is designed to appeal to your target audience and that it's reflective of your brand is the first step you need to make your business competitive.

Your website should be mobile friendly with the modern-day operating systems and browsers. The fact is that there are more mobile phones in the planet than the total number of people. This is clear evidence that people use the phone or a tablet device to do most things whenever and wherever they are.

Easy to navigate websites are a plus as a visitor can find products and/or services in a hustle-free manner. Always mark important content clearly and prominently and have updated information.

Including the most frequently asked questions in your website is crucial as it answers possible questions your web visitor may have upfront therefore helps in clearing out all the reasons that may hold them back from contacting or purchasing from you. This section is usually very fundamental though it may not be applicable to all businesses depending on the nature of your business. Having your policies easy to find (for instance if you are in the shipping business etc.) makes things a lot easier for users to read and understand the terms and conditions before doing business with you. Always be transparent, it's an indisputable moral code.

While it may be cheap and easy, cheap and quick to create a website using free Online tools, it's worth noting that they do not support Search Engine and are not customizable. If you are serious about creating a solid website with a return on investment for your business, I highly recommend that you consider hiring a developer. It may be expensive but it's always worth the value and effort.

Thing to consider when hiring a developer

a. Review their website and evaluate it because your website should achieve its goal and for a developer to have a good marketing eye is a plus.

b. Check at the recency of their work as this will give you an overview on how the developer stays up to date with trending technologies.

c. Look at their portfolio as it will give you an overview of the quality of the sites they've done.

d. Read through their testimonials and reviews. Feel free to ask and visit the developer's website and LinkedIn profile and see most of it.

2) Search Engine Optimization (SEO)

This simply means where you rank on an Online search after a visitor types something on their browser is called Search Engine Optimization (SEO). Most businesses today either do not understand or ignore this part. It has and will always be an expensive mistake for businesses that take it for granted because it's a great way to generate revenue by attracting customers. The fact is that when a potential customer goes Online and they cannot find your business, you lose a sale instantly. Every day, millions of customers go Online to either buy or find information of something they want to buy, make your business visible by promoting it online. Most businesses today are suffering the loss of huge profit margins just because of this.

For instance, you have a business that sells something like beauty products and you have a website for your business but when a potential client searches on Search Engine like Google, Bing, Yandex, and/or Yahoo something like say "where can I find best beauty products nearby? "and you don't appear on the first page, guess what would have just happened? You lost a sale! It's important to note that very few visitors navigate to the second or even the third page once they miss or find something, they are looking for on the first page. That's a problem that you need it fixed.

Whether it's paid results or organic results, *search is the most valuable real estate Online*. That said, SEO is always an ongoing effort and so you should always provide professionals with enough time to demonstrate success on your site. It takes a lot of time and work, and expertise come at a premium. When done right, it can have an impressive Return on Investment and you should always involve SEO early on. If you already have a website, I highly recommend that you get a professional to do an SEO site audit for your site and come up with a strategy development for your website.

If your website isn't good enough in some kind of way, it's a guarantee that you will definitely fall further behind in this competitive digital era even as the landscape continues to evolve. Even worse, if your website isn't optimized, you are already behind!

3) **Social Media Marketing**

Nowadays, people of all ages right from millennials to baby boomers consume social media more like candy as it evolves to visual marketing. With the use of mobile phones, billions of people around the world consume social media every minute of the day.

There are many social media platforms today and more are still to come up in the future as technology continues to evolve. It's therefore important to identify the ones that work for you best depending on the product and/or service you are offering and also your target market. For instance, if you are selling clothing wear, it could be best to use short and informative videos either as an advertisement on YouTube or you could include it in your website or do both. In all cases, you can drive traffic to your website when done right. The better the marketing, the more visibility your website will get.

Nowadays, people tend to hang out more on social media platforms and this gives entrepreneurs a much bigger chance to reach their customers. Different social media platforms have different forums that people contribute to different topics. Just by participating in those discussions, you can drive a lot of traffic to your website or your street address, if that's what you want.

When social media is done right, it has a huge potential to change your business because it has a high return on investment although it requires a lot of good strategy, creativity and a bit of luck. It's important to particularly take note of what kind of people are using each social media platform. Different sites tend to attract different genders, different age groups, different geographies and social media particularly can be a very powerful tool as long as it's used wisely.

On the other hand, if done wrong, it backfires as it ends up bringing unwanted attention which may be detrimental for your business brand.

Tips on getting more followers on social media:

i.   Always post valuable content that resonates with your target audience.

ii. Be bold and express your feelings and opinions, whether right or wrong it's your platform. Take a stand!

iii. Embed a video or attach an image to every post, it doubles engagements.

iv.   Compliment other people's post when you find them good, credit the source, re-share other people's posts and give them kudos. This is practicing good karma/goodwill.

v.   Have fun! This way you will be more enthusiastic, look for more stuff and post more.

4) **Email marketing**

This is an old way of marketing but still very relevant in today's world. Long ago, marketers would focus more on generating leads but the game has changed today. The main interest is to generate quality leads for the business that can convert. Conversion is an action of purchase. Most businesses still use this especially the ones that sell products and/or services Online. They could be digital products, selling tickets, bookings, sign ups, or even physical products on an e-commerce site. With fixed conversions, you can increase revenue without increasing traffic.

This works in relation to websites and social medias. The best way to collect quality leads for your business is through promoting Online and having a real and an appropriate landing page for whatever you are trying to do and/or achieve. There are different types of designs for landing pages depending on whatever you are trying to achieve.

The standard general requirements for your landing page are that it should have a call to action button. This is a button prompting visitor to take action. Explanation of the offer, compelling headline, a logo, your privacy policy, contact information and a valid SSL Certificate should also be included.

You email campaigns on the other hand should have a message with a headline, a verbiage, a call to action button, sender's email address, and a logo of your brand. It's important to note that different activities may require different requirements and some are regulated by the law. If you are green in this area, it's best recommended that you consult and seek advice from a professional marketer before starting off.

5) **Artificial Intelligence**

This is the crucial part in today's and in the future generation of technology. A lot of modern digital platforms are beginning to embrace it fully. For instance, e-commerce sites are now the big-time beneficiary of this because when one shops in a site, it has improved suggestions of other products that you can shop and it also tells you what other people who bought the same product as you also bought. It's seen even in membership economy sites like Netflix where when you watch a movie, it shows you relevant suggestions that would best suite you. Artificial Intelligence is also powering so many machines and devices too. For instance, today's robots are being powered by AI including the news reporter that has human facial expressions and also the robotic waiter that serves people not only it has human facial expressions but also has courtesy.

One of the most crucial bits that will help you in forecasting and determining the success of your business is collecting data. Measuring data could include the number of visitors', their location, visit duration and their visit points. Always track data as much as possible as it always gives you insights on improving experience, finding new opportunities, and discontinuing failing ideas. There are different pools of collecting data in your website like using analytics and even in sales for instance by using customer relations management systems and many more depending on what you are trying to achieve.

Data is today's oil. Good luck in digital marketing!

NEXT STEPS

As you continue growing your business more and more, it's a good idea that you decide to take a charitable cause; something you believe in that will change the world, as it's always very valuable for businesses to have something deeper rather than just making profits. This usually adds up more energy and motivation to the business. Nothing brings people together like working together for a good cause because it will have a powerful effect on the culture of your business as it will even unify employees for, they are working together for a greater good. You will even start attracting the kind of employees that you want to work for you. A cause will increase the level of employee engagement since as a business owner, you care a great deal about your business, and you'll probably always be the one that cares the most about your business. When you have a cause, you'll see that level of caring about the business success starts to increase because they now feel like they're actually doing something for the business to succeed, and that they are actually making a difference in the world. It will also increase awareness of your brand as you may couple up with other renowned non-profit organizations that will help in boosting your awareness. Immeasurable benefits (karma or goodwill) come along with serving others.

Summary

You need to build a business steadily and consistently such that you will have enjoy it and have a wonderful life. Take advantage of technology as a tool for your business and use it to your advantage in growing your business and remember to always read and learn new industry and market trends. As a business owner, you should focus much on the success of the business and not it's perfection.

QUESTIONS:

1. Data is today's _____

2. What are the things to consider before hiring a developer?

3. State and explain some digital trends today

4. Name some tips on how to gain more followers in social media

5. Name some objectives that your organization should have

6. Search results are the most _____ real estate
_____

BIBLIOGRAPHY

Sramana Mitra. (2008). Entrepreneur Journey (Volume 1)

Peter A. High. (2014). World Class IT Strategy

Dave Crenshaw. (2013). The Focused Business: How Entrepreneurs can Triumph Over Chaos

Rudolph Rosenberg. (2008). And Somehow, We Survive.

ABOUT THE AUTHOR

DENNIS MBUGUA is a serial entrepreneur. He's passionate about helping companies grow using today's technology and he's also a business and a tech consultant. His skills, talents and experiences have made him gain a lot of hands-on expertise and knowledge with regards to business and technology trends. He is the Founder of Starlaunch Technology.

Company website: https://www.starlaunch.org/
Personal website: https://www.dennismbugua.online/

www.ingramcontent.com/pod-product-compliance
Lightning Source LLC
Chambersburg PA
CBHW030729180526
45157CB00008BA/3101